ASTRA'S DREAM FRIENDS

GRACE BREWSTER

Copyright © 2025 Grace Brewster
All rights reserved.
No part of this book may be reproduced, stored in a retrieval system, or transmitted in any form or by any means – electronic, mechanical, photocopying, recording, or otherwise – without the prior written permission of the author, except for brief quotations in a review.
This is a work of fiction. Any resemblance to actual events or persons, living or dead, is purely coincidental.
Illustrations created in collaboration with AI-generated artwork.

First Edition: 2025
ISBN: 978-1-0696945-2-2
Independently Published

Dedication
For every child who dreams of friends,
may you always remember: love travels through dreams
and never fades with the morning light.

At bedtime, Astra snuggled under her blanket.
"She whispered to the stars, 'I wonder what you'll show me tonight.'"

She drifted into sleep, and just like always...
Zoom!

Her spaceship lifted off and there they were! Her pink and blue alien friends waved from their glowing ship.

They played hide and seek behind cotton-candy planets.

They bounced on dream clouds and painted moons with stardust.

But the next morning...
Plop.
 There was a soft pink alien plush on Astra's pillow.

Astra blinked. "Were you always here?" she asked. The toy didn't answer... but it smiled just like her dream friend. She gave her a name – Luna.

That night, the blue alien whispered,
"We left you a little piece of us... so you'll never feel alone." Her name was Nova.

Astra woke up and found the blue plush too. Now both sat on her nightstand, quietly glowing.

Each night, Astra flew back to the stars.

Each morning, something magical stayed behind —
 like a giggle in the pillow, or sparkles near the window.

And even when she was awake, Astra knew:
Her dream friends, Luna and Nova, were never far away.

Because when love travels through dreams... it always finds a way.

✨ About the Author ✨

Grace Brewster believes that stories are starlight — they remind us where we come from and guide us when the night feels dark. She writes gentle bedtime tales filled with wonder, imagination, and a sprinkle of cosmic magic to help little dreamers feel safe, loved, and connected to the universe.
When she's not writing, Grace loves exploring new places, watching the stars, and sharing laughter that feels like it belongs to the whole galaxy.

🌟 Also by Grace Brewster 🌟
📖 Astra's Starry Dream
🌻 The Giants and the Sunflowers
🌙 Astra & The Rainbow Bridge
🔺 The Pyramids from the Stars

www.ingramcontent.com/pod-product-compliance
Lightning Source LLC
LaVergne TN
LVHW072100070426
835508LV00002B/194